HANGING
WITH
VAMPIRES

HANGING WITH
VAMPIRES

By Insha Fitzpatrick

Illustrations by Lilla Bölecz

A TOTALLY FACTUAL
FIELD GUIDE TO THE
SUPERNATURAL

QUIRK BOOKS
PHILADELPHIA

Library of Congress Cataloging-in-Publication Data
Names: Fitzpatrick, Insha, author. | Bölecz, Lilla, illustrator.
Title: Hanging with vampires : a totally factual field guide to the supernatural /
   by Insha Fitzpatrick ; illustrations by Lilla Bölecz.
Description: Philadelphia, PA : Quirk Books, [2023] | Series: A totally factual field
   guide to the supernatural ; 1 | Includes bibliographical references. | Audience:
   Ages 8-12 years | Audience: Grades 4-6 | Summary: "An illustrated nonfiction
   guide to vampires in history, legend, and pop culture"—Provided by publisher.
Identifiers: LCCN 2022033757 (print) | LCCN 2022033758 (ebook) |
   ISBN 9781683693413 (Paperback) | ISBN 9781683693420 (eBook)
Subjects: LCSH: Vampires—Juvenile literature.
Classification: LCC GR830.V3 F58 2023 (print) | LCC GR830.V3 (ebook) |
   DDC 398.21—dc23/eng/20220720
LC record available at https://lccn.loc.gov/2022033757
LC ebook record available at https://lccn.loc.gov/2022033758

ISBN: 978-1-68369-341-3

Printed in China

Typeset in Black Magic, Freight, Fright Night, and Wolfsbane

Designed by Andie Reid
Illustrations by Lilla Bölecz
Production management by John J. McGurk

Quirk Books
215 Church Street
Philadelphia, PA 19106
quirkbooks.com

10 9 8 7 6 5 4 3 2 1

To Geraldine,
the vampire queen, and to
all the lil supernaturalists,
stay spooky!

CONTENTS

Introduction

ARE VAMPIRES REAL?

Welcome! Whether you picked up this field guide out of sheer boredom or keen curiosity, let me be the first to welcome you on your journey into the unknown. If you love terrifying tales and bone-chilling legends, you're in the right place. If you hate all that stuff, that's cool, too! Stick around. This field guide has it all: Science! History! Gross facts! Not-so-gross facts! Cute bats! A really good garlic bread recipe! Seriously, don't go. Come back! Please!

UH . . . WHO ARE YOU?

Excellent question, hypothetical reader! I'm your guide to the weird world of the supernatural. In this book, I'll cover everything there is to know about vampires, and then some. It's like the saying goes: knowledge is power against bloodsucking children of the night.

THE ELEPHANT—ER, VAMPIRE IN THE ROOM

Vampires?! *Are they even real?* Well, the answer is: yes and no.

When you think of the classic vampire, you're probably imagining a spooky undead being who stalks the night, looking for their next innocent human to suck blood from. Or perhaps you're imagining a sparkly, glamorous vampire who goes to high school. Maybe this vampire can turn into a bat, likes to sleep in a coffin, and has fangs pointy enough to make a dentist faint.

That kind of vampire, the vampires in books and movies and our imaginations? They don't exist. At least, not in the real world. You're not going to run into a vampire sucking on a blood bag like it's a juice box while you're walking the dog or biking to school.

But what if I told you that there is more to vampires than just a guy in a cape who can turn into a bat? The vampire legend has to come from *somewhere*, right? That's where things get interesting.

Vampire lore has its roots in real-life history, science, and culture.

The same goes for just about any supernatural legend. There's a story behind everything. You just have to know where to look.

WHAT'S IN THIS THING?

In this guide, we're going to bust that coffin wide open and shine a light on the mystery of how the vampire legend got started and how vampires became such a big deal. We'll dig into all the basics with Vampires 101, study up on the history of vampires, and meet terrifying vampire-like supernatural creatures from all around the world!

The world is a spooky, weird, and awesome place. This field guide is here to help you on your journey as you explore the supernatural. So, whenever you're ready, let's go! And by *go*, I mean keep reading. This is a book, after all.

Dig Out the Dictionary!

What counts as supernatural? Merriam-Webster defines *supernatural* as "departing from what is usual or normal, especially so as to appear to transcend the laws of nature." In this guide, when I say *supernatural*, I mean any being, creature, or phenomenon that isn't deemed "normal" or scientifically explainable. Examples of supernatural beings include vampires, ghosts, werewolves, merfolk, and zombies.

Chapter 1

VAMPIRES 101

There are more
things in heaven and earth,
Horatio, than are dreamt
of in your philosophy.

—Hamlet, *Hamlet*,
Act I, scene v

So What IS a Vampire, Anyway?

Since I haven't scared you off (yet), we'll start our voyage into the world of vampires with the basics. How do you spot a vampire? Where do vampires hang out? What do vampires drink? (Spoiler alert: they drink blood.) We'll get to all that and more in Vampires 101!

HOW TO IDENTIFY A VAMPIRE

First things first, you need to know how to identify a vampire! Now, picture a vampire. Using my psychic abilities, I'm guessing the first thing that comes to mind is a pale and brooding man with dark, slicked-back hair and a long cape—not a Superman cape, but a velvety black cape with red lining. And of course, this spooky figure has two pointy fangs, perfect for sucking blood.

Did I get it right? If I did, you were picturing the classic vampire look! This particular vampire style comes to mind first because it's what vampires in eighteenth- and nineteenth-century literature looked like. Think Dracula from Bram Stoker's 1897 novel titled (surprise, surprise) *Dracula*. And because these vampires of ye olde literature were sometimes based on real-life (and super-rich) people from that time period, we tend to think of vampires as wearing fancy, old-fashioned clothes.

Read All About It

The classic vampire look was established by playwright Hamilton Deane, who adapted Bram Stoker's novel *Dracula* for the stage in 1924. This look was further cemented in our collective imaginations when Bela Lugosi donned a cape, fangs, and a mysterious air of elegance in Universal Studios' movie retelling of Stoker's novel in 1931.

If you're thinking of someone scarier, you might be picturing a reanimated corpse with fangs. After all, vampires are technically un-dead! Take Count Orlok from the 1922 silent film *Nosferatu*—with his long fingernails, pointy fangs, and menacing looks, the corpse-like Count Orlok is a terrifying figure to behold.

"Hang on," you might say. "What if I wasn't picturing the classic vampire or a creepy living corpse?" Well, you might be imagining a more modern style of vampire from a recent movie, TV show, or book. As Aubrey Sherman writes in the book *Vampires: The Myths, Legends, and Lore,* "Your idea of vampires will vary depending on what you've seen or read." Plus, according to vampire lore, just about anyone can be turned into a vampire, which means vampires can really look like anyone at all!

Long story short? Vampires don't have a singular, distinct appearance. Our understanding of legends and stories is always changing with the times. What we think a vampire looks like is influenced by the times we live in, the books we read, the movies we watch, and so much more. The real question is: what makes a vampire a vampire? The most basic vampire attributes are . . .

- Has pointy fangs for bloodsucking
- Drinks primarily human blood
- Has an affinity for bats, may be capable of shapeshifting into one
- Is undead and (almost) immortal

Got it? Good. Now that we've covered the basics, let's take a deeper look at common vampire traits and classic vampire lore. You never know when this might come in handy!

b. night vision

a. fangs

c. weak against the sun

e. bat friend

d. stylish cape (for drama)

HOW TO IDENTIFY A VAMPIRE

Fangs

Vampires use their fangs to feed. Depending on the vampire, they might have *retractable* fangs, which means they can hide away their fangs . . . kind of like how cats can retract their claws! Since a vampire's fangs can be retracted, you can't rely on fangs alone to identify a vampire.

According to Science

Speaking of retractable . . . Moray eels have not one but two sets of jaws. Their second jaw is a retractable jaw, called a pharyngeal jaw, that allows them to drag their prey in and fully swallow it after the initial chomp! Another creature with retractable features is the viper. Vipers are solenoglyphous snakes, which means they have long, hollow fangs that they use to give their prey deep puncture wounds and inject venom. How do those fangs fit into their mouths? They fold up to lie flat against their upper jaw and swing down when it's time to strike! One example of this type of snake is the famously dangerous rattlesnake.

Drinking Blood

Vampires may not eat regular food like we humans do, but they've got to consume something to keep going. The ideal vampire meal is fresh human blood, straight from the source. According to legend, a vampire might even hypnotize their victims in order to drink their blood. Watch out!

According to Science

Vampire bats are hematophagous—they feed on blood for food. Other animals that practice hematophagy include fleas, one genus of moth, leeches, bedbugs, oxpecker birds, vampire finches, lamprey fish, and, my personal worst enemy, mosquitoes.

Bats and Shapeshifting

Ever seen a colony of bats take flight? As nocturnal creatures, bats were associated with demons and witchcraft during medieval times. When Bram Stoker linked bats with Dracula in his novel, that sealed the deal—bats are a vampire's best friend. Some stories give vampires the ability to shapeshift into wolves and bats, and sometimes even smoke or mist.

Immortality

Vampires are considered undead and (mostly) immortal. In *Dracula*, Bram Stoker defines the undead as supernatural beings who "cannot die but must go on age after age." The undead are dead, but don't act like it! Other examples of the undead are zombies, banshees, and poltergeists.

No Reflection

Look in the mirror. You're most likely reflected in it, and if you're not, then you should really clean your mirror. It's said that vampires aren't reflected in mirrors because . . . well, there's two popular explanations:

1 According to vampire lore, vampires don't have souls. In the past people believed that you needed a soul to show up in the mirror. If someone can't be seen in a mirror—proceed with caution!

2 Old mirrors were backed with silver, which people believed could ward off various supernatural creatures including vampires and werewolves.

Ye Olde History

Back when vampire hunters and townspeople dug up the graves of people suspected to be vampires, one of the signs to look for was if the corpse's nails and hair kept growing. What these people didn't know was that when bodies decay, the skin shrivels or shrinks. This makes it look like the corpse's nails and hair are continuing to grow after death.

Supernatural Powers

Once someone is turned into a vampire, they may discover newfound supernatural abilities. Vampires are often depicted as having super-strength, powers of hypnotism, and lightning-quick reflexes that could give an Olympian a run for their money. New vampires might also might gain a heightened sense of hearing, sight, and smell.

Nocturnality

Like bats, vampires are famously creatures of the night. Typically, they sleep during the day and hunt during the night, which means they're nocturnal—they love when the sun goes down. Sunlight is said to burn and even destroy vampires. But in modern media, vampires are becoming more chill with hanging out in the sun. This is a great example of how, as our perceptions and values change, so do the stories that get told about vampires.

According to Science

You may not be a vampire* but if you've ever been sunburned, then you know what it's like to be one. Sunburn happens when your skin gets exposed to too much UV radiation from the sun. This can cause long-term health problems like skin cancer, so it's super important to wear sunscreen if you're spending lots of time outside. Tell your friends and enemies: wear sunscreen!

*At least, I hope you're not a vampire. If you are . . . awkward.

HOW DOES A VAMPIRE BECOME A VAMPIRE?

Accounts vary! Depending on the legend, a person might turn into a vampire for all sorts of different reasons, such as:

- If they practiced sorcery or witchcraft
- If a vampire killed them
- If they were cursed at birth or were born during a new moon
- If their mother stared at a vampire while pregnant
- If their mother didn't eat the right amount of salt while pregnant

As you can see, there's some pretty interesting ways people can turn into vampires according to different stories. The classic method you've probably heard of is a vampire biting a human, and instead of just feeding on them, giving the human some of their blood . . . and boom! The human dies and reawakens as a brand-new member of the fang club with a craving for blood.

HOME IS WHERE THE VAMP LIVES

Let's discuss where vampires are found. And no, you can't just search for a vampire on Google Maps. Let's take a look at what we know:

1 **Vampires tend to keep to themselves.** Why? Well, vampires can live for thousands of years, and being immortal is lonely business! Plus, vampires generally have to keep their vampirehood a secret. Wouldn't want a vampire hunter showing up on their doorstep, right?

2 **Vampires are often super rich.** Okay, this one is a bit of a stretch, but stick with me. Historically, some fictional vampires were based on or loosely inspired by real-life people who just so happened to be rich—sometimes even royalty! That's why when you think of a classic vampire name, you tend to think of "Count" this or "Queen" that.

3 **Vampires need a source of food.** Since vampires feed on humans, they can't exactly survive on the moon. Vampires need to be close enough to where humans live to go out and feed.

4 **Vampires sleep during the day.** If you've been paying attention—and I sure hope you have!—you know that vampires are nocturnal and generally can't stand the sun. That means they need to stay someplace safe, where they won't be disturbed while they snooze.

Where a vampire lives can vary depending on the time period and where they are. Take Count Dracula: he lives in a massive castle in Transylvania, with spiderwebs and spiky towers galore. That's pretty standard for a vampire. However, some modern vampires don't go for the grandeur of a big castle. In the 1985 film *Fright Night*, the vampire Jerry Dandrige lives in an average, everyday suburban home. If you were a vampire, where would you want to live? I think I'd live in an Ikea—plenty of beds to snooze on!

Read All About It

Bram Stoker's Count Dracula lives in a castle in Transylvania, a historical Eastern European region in what is now Romania. But did you know that Stoker based the castle on real locations? Count Dracula's lair is inspired by Bran Castle and Poenari Castle in Romania. In fact, people visit Bran Castle every year to take tours and score vampire-themed memorabilia.

Sweet Dreams

Speaking of snoozing . . . Like humans, vampires need their beauty sleep! Vampires traditionally rest their sleepy heads in a coffin. (FYI, coffins and caskets are two different things! Coffins are hexagonal wooden boxes with six sides to them and a removable lid, while caskets have a four-sided, rectangular base and a hinged lid.)

Read All About It

Another thing you might've heard about vampire sleeping habits is that they sleep on soil from their homeland. Who came up with this legend? You guessed it—Bram Stoker. Count Dracula had to bring boxes of his native soil with him wherever he moved!

Hey, check it out—you've survived Vampire 101! Congrats! Give yourself a high five. Well, I guess that would just be clapping. Go find someone else to high-five!

So You Want to Spot a Vampire

Totally hypothetically speaking, if you met a vampire, do you think you'd be able to figure out if they were a vampire? It's not like they walk around holding a sign that says HI, I'M A VAMPIRE. Just in case, here's a handy cheat sheet to help you figure out if there's a vampire in your area.

Let's set the scene. A new neighbor just moved into the huge spooky mansion up on the hill. Strange things have been happening, and you've got this sneaking suspicion that your neighbor is secretly a vampire! Ask yourself the following questions.

1 **Are people in your neighborhood starting to act . . . weird?** And I don't mean weird as in a quirky personality trait—everyone's different, and that rocks. By weird, I mean "preyed upon by a vampire." Are people acting like they've been hypnotized? Are turtlenecks and sleepwalking suddenly the latest fashion? Has anyone said to you, "Wow, I met a vampire yesterday, and they totally sucked my blood!" If so, there might just be a vampire in your area.

2 **Are there suddenly a lot of bats in your area?** Your neighborhood might be a hot spot for bats. Three cheers for wildlife! Then again, maybe the bats came with your new vampire neighbor . . .

3 **Does your neighbor only go out at night?** If so, chances are they're just a night owl, someone who works a night shift, or a graduate school student. But if you also catch your neighbor going "ssssss!" at the sun and acting like daylight will literally set their skin on fire, that's a vampire sign right there.

4 **Does your neighbor refuse to consume human food?** This is your chance to do a little detective work. Ask them what they like to eat. If their response is something suspicious such as "I like to eat normal human food, not the fresh, crimson blood of a living person" or "I'd kill for a glass of blood," run!

5 **Are bloodless animal bodies mysteriously appearing?** First of all, ew, don't touch that. Second of all, you might have a vampire in your neighborhood. Or the world's biggest mosquito. Or a serial killer. Or a chupacabra (more on this in Chapter 4). Exercise caution!

So, in this (again, totally made-up) scenario, if your answers to all five of these questions are yes, you might have a vampire on your hands. Depending on the vampire, this might not be a problem. If this vampire is super chill and doesn't prey on humans, then you're good. But if this vampire has an insatiable thirst for human blood, you'll want to be prepared. In the next chapter, we'll uncover a vampire's weaknesses and how you can defeat a vampire. Turn the page . . . if you dare!

Chapter 2

HOW TO FIGHT A VAMPIRE (AND WIN)

> Hey, slaying is what we're built for. If you're not enjoying it, you're doing something wrong.
>
> —Faith, *Buffy the Vampire Slayer*

Well, well, well. You think you can go up against a vampire and win? Ha! Not a chance. But armed with knowledge and a ton of garlic, you might just be able to take on a vampire. I know what you're thinking: "It's easy! Can't I just stick them with the pointy end?" Nah, it's a little more complicated than that. As we learned in Chapter 1, there are many different kinds of vampires. But there are also many ways to defeat a vampire. The key is understanding a vampire's strengths and weaknesses.

VAMPIRE STRENGTHS

We know the most common strengths of vampires, but there are even cooler ones that we haven't sunk our teeth into yet.

Hypnosis

Hypnosis is when someone is put into a sort of trance that makes them more vulnerable to being told how to act. If a vampire stared deep into your eyes, hypnotized you, and said, "Flap your wings like a bat!," you'd do it. If a vampire tries to hypnotize you, keep your mind sharp and try not to let them get inside your brain! Think about something totally different: brick walls, cheese puffs, or your pet.

Beauty

Vampires are often portrayed as drop-dead gorgeous—it's part of their charm. Some people in ye olden days (and unfortunately, ye modern days, too) believed that being beautiful was a sign of virtue. If you were good-looking, you were a good person, too! Obviously, that isn't actually true. Beauty isn't everything. It's what's on the inside that counts, like your major organs and your personality!

Healing

Vampires have some fang-tastic abilities to heal themselves! They're basically immortal, after all. Pretty much only being staked or decapitated will keep a vampire down.

VAMPIRE WEAKNESSES

According to famous vampire legends and folklore, there are some surefire ways to defeat a member of the fang club.

Wooden Stakes

No, not steaks. We're talking wooden stakes, a.k.a. a piece of wood sharpened to a point and a must-have for any vampire hunter! In vampire tales, stakes are often wielded to pierce through a vampire's heart. Weird, right? The origins of this practice trace back to the medieval idea that staking a corpse would pin it to the ground so it couldn't rise from the dead.

Garlic

In European folklore, garlic was said to drive away various supernatural beings, including demons, werewolves, and, of course, vampires! It was also used to ward off curses like the evil eye. People would hang garlic over their door, rub it on their windows, or wear it around their necks, like a fabulous (and pungent!) necklace.

According to Science

Even though vampires can't stand garlic, garlic can be healthy for you! Garlic is said to be anti-inflammatory (prevents swelling), antimicrobial (bye, germs), and an antioxidant (helps slow cell damage). If you crush garlic, it releases allicin. Allicin is why garlic is a pest repellent and why it's so fragrant.

Sunlight

As we've covered, vampires are not fans of the sun. Where did this belief come from? There's a variety of possible explanations. One explanation: nighttime was associated with the evil and unknown,

while the sunlight was considered holy and good—and therefore bad for vampires.

Invitations

Before a vampire can kick up their feet and rest their fangs in your home, they have to be invited in first! Vampires cannot enter a home or space without an invitation from the person who lives there. (But once they get an invitation, they're able to come and go from that place as they please.)

Holy Water

In several religions, water is used in rituals for blessing, cleansing, and purification. Water blessed by a religious figure or a clergy member, like a priest, is considered holy water. Since vampires were thought of as impure creatures, people believed holy water could be used against them.

Holy or Religious Items

Vampires were considered evil, and how do you fight evil? With evil! Just kidding: with holy stuff. Various holy and religious items were added to the classic vampire-hunter arsenal.

The Vampire Will Be Televised

There've been some pretty weird weapons used to slay the vampires in film and TV. In Interview with the Vampire, Louis uses a scythe to cut through vampires. A wheel impales Count Dracula in *Dracula A.D. 1972*. And in *The Lost Boys*, Nanook the dog knocks a vampire into a tub of holy water and garlic!

TOOLS OF THE VAMPIRE-HUNTING TRADE

First rule for dealing with the supernatural? Always be ready. If, in some bizarre and improbable turn of events, you have to fight a vampire, we at Field Guide to the Supernatural HQ have just the thing for you . . .

NOW INTRODUCING:

THE FANG-TACTIC VAMPIRE TOOL KIT

Sticking it to vampires has never been easier with the new and improved vampire tool kit, FANG-TACTIC! If you're not into driving a stake through a vampire's heart (ew), we hear you. With this tool kit, you'll have everything you need to take on a vampire... and win. What's in it?

1. **GARLIC BREAD:** Pack some garlic bread to feed your hunger and to shoo away that pesky vampire!

2. **COMPACT MIRROR:** No need to pack your bedroom mirror, just bring a travel-size mirror! Perfect for checking for vampires and whether you've got spinach in your teeth.

3. **SMARTPHONE AND/OR FLASHLIGHT:** You can't carry around sunlight, but you can carry around a flashlight! The flashlight function on a smartphone, if you have one, will do in a pinch.

4. **SPRAY BOTTLE FILLED WITH HOLY WATER:** Don't have holy water? Easy. Just (politely!) ask your local priest, clergyperson, or anyone religious in your life to bless some water for you and,

ta-da, (unofficial) holy water! A good spritz will make vampires flee for their coffins.

(5) **WATER BOTTLE FILLED WITH REGULAR WATER:** This one's for you. Staying hydrated is important! (Fun fact: About 50 to 60 percent of your body is made up of water.)

(6) **PONCHO:** Listen, dealing with the supernatural can get pretty messy, and we don't want your nice shirt (or your nice sweater, dress, overalls, pajamas, etc.) to get all gross, right? If a vampire spontaneously combusts in the sunlight or a bat poops on you, you're (literally) covered.

(7) **THIS GUIDE:** You can pretend this guide is a holy religious text. Just hold it up and yell "Begone with you!" to ward off vampires. (Hopefully, they won't know the difference.) Plus, it never hurts to pack a good book to read.

But wait, you might say, where's all the vampire-killing stuff? You know, like a razor-sharp stake or a magic sword for beheading a living corpse. Here's the thing: according to legend, vampires are super strong, super fast, and can be super dangerous. In the totally hypothetical scenario that you encounter a vampire, your best bet is to ward it off and run. It's better to be smart than to be stabby!

Want to beat a vampire? The secret is to outsmart them and use their weaknesses against them. One example of an antivampire strategy: hide in a house with big windows and hang out until it's daytime (a.k.a. vampire roasting time). Remember, a vampire can't enter a home without an invitation. When the sun is just about to rise, it's go time—invite your vampire nemesis inside. Carefully and quickly lure them to a window, bust open those shades, and the sunlight will dust that vampire right into the carpet! You might want to have the vacuum handy.

But that's just one way of taking on a vampire. When facing the unknown, your best strategy is . . . to know it! For us, that means taking it all the way back. We're about to go digging up the history of vampires! In the next chapter, we'll (metaphorically) unbury some coffins and uncover the bloody truth. But first, it's snack time.

Bat Breath Garlic Bread

In addition to being a world-class supernatural guide, I'm also a supernatural . . . ly amazing home chef! Here's a recipe that does the double duty of filling your stomach and warding off vampires. (If you're a young chef, please have an adult help you with this delicious snack. Be careful, and stay safe!)

INGREDIENTS:

1 baguette or loaf French bread
   (any hefty loaf of bread will do)
4 cloves garlic, minced (if you really like garlic, add more!)
½ cup unsalted butter, softened to room temperature
1 tablespoon chopped fresh parsley (1 tablespoon dried parsley
   works too, if you don't have fresh)
½ teaspoon kosher salt (or a bit less if using table salt)
Optional: ¼ cup grated mozzarella, cheddar, or parmesan
   cheese

HOW TO MAKE AND BAKE:

1 Preheat oven to 400°F. Be careful, that's blazing hot!

2 Line a large baking sheet with foil or parchment paper. This makes for easier cleanup.

3 Cut bread into 1-inch slices. If you're feeling crafty, slice a piece into the shape of a bat or a moon. Just be careful with that knife!

4 In a bowl combine garlic, butter, parsley, and salt.

5 Spread a small amount of the butter mixture onto each slice of bread. Place the bread butter side up on the lined baking sheet and carefully slide the sheet into the oven. Set a timer for 10–15 minutes!

6 When time is up or when you see the bread is golden brown and the butter is bubbling on the top (also, you'll smell that garlicky goodness), pull on your oven mitts and carefully remove the hot baking sheet from the oven and place it on a cooling rack. While the garlic bread is still hot, sprinkle with cheese, if you so desire. (I like to throw on some parm!)

Bon appétit! A delicious recipe that'll knock a vampire right out if they catch a whiff of your amazing, garlicky breath!

Chapter 3

VAMPIRES THROUGH THE AGES

Every family
has a legacy, and
this is mine.

—Hope Mikaelson,
The Originals

Urgh, history is *bo*-ring. I don't need a history lesson!" you might be thinking. Here's a little secret about history: it's gross, weird, terrifying, and deeply cool. After all, history is the story of humankind, and humans are anything but boring. I promise you'll want to stick around for this—stake my heart and hope to die, splash some holy water in my eye.

LEGENDARY BLOODSUCKERS

How did the vampire legend get its start? We can speculate that the vampire legend has roots in stories from countries including Greece, India, Egypt, and Ukraine. Let's meet a few famous bloodsuckers from myth, legend, and folklore.

Lamia, The Vengeful Queen

According to ancient Greek mythology, there was a woman named Lamia. She was a beautiful Libyan queen who gained the attention of Zeus, the god of sky and thunder, and soon became his lover. When Hera, the goddess of marriage (and Zeus's wife!), found out that Lamia was pregnant with Zeus's child, she grew angry and stole Lamia's children. Whenever Lamia gave birth, Hera would take the baby away or make Lamia kill the child herself. A Greek god's wrath is no joke!

Lamia was filled with rage at Hera's cruelty, and that rage turned to madness. She began stealing children away from their mothers, just like Hera had stolen her children, and devouring them.

In later stories, the lamiai were child-devouring monsters with the upper body of a woman and the lower body of a serpent. Some legends described the lamiai as shapeshifters who could transform themselves into beautiful women to lure men to their doom. (If you read a lot of mythology, legends, or old tales, you'll notice that many stories talk about beautiful women being the downfall of men. Yeah, it's kind of sexist!)

Ye Olde History

In ancient Greece, mothers and caretakers would tell their children that if they misbehaved, Lamia would come in the night and steal them away. Well, that's one way to scare kids into behaving!

The Upior

Time for a spooky story! Get some marshmallows, chocolate, and graham crackers and gather around the fire. I'm going to tell you the story of . . . the upior.

Once upon a time, an unnamed woman from a small village was suspected of being a witch. The woman died suddenly and was later buried. Days later, she rose from her grave as a horrifying corpse. She had transformed into an upior!

The upior attacked the villagers at night, squeezing them in a deadly embrace and drinking their blood. The attacks would mysteriously stop during the day. To save themselves, the villagers exhumed the upior's grave to figure out what exactly was going on . . . and discovered that the upior had a blood-soaked rag stuffed into her mouth.

The villagers knew what they needed to do: they drove a sharp stake through the corpse's chest. But the upior didn't die. That night, she returned to the village, using the stake to attack the villagers and their dogs. Only when the villagers burned the upior's corpse were they free from her bloody reign of terror.

BOO!

After hearing that story, you might think I made it up. Did I? Yes and no. The story I just told you is adapted from Slavic folklore about the upior. So what's an upior? Is it some kind of vampire? And weren't we just talking about a monster from Greek mythology? Well, my dear reader, this will all make sense in a sec.

Vampire folklore goes all the way back to ancient Greece and beyond. But it was the legends of Eastern Europe that really began to send shivers down our spines, with folklore that emerged from various cultural traditions and beliefs. These terrifying tales that cropped up throughout Eastern Europe, especially Russia, Poland, Romania (where Transylvania is!), and Ukraine, led to the spooky vampire tales we know today.

One of those tales? The legend of the upior. Now try this: say "upior" three times. Did saying it remind you of another word? Like, perhaps, "vampire"? The upior is just one of many pieces of folklore that make up the vampire puzzle.

The upior (who also goes by upiór, upor, upiorz or upiroy) is the name for a vampire in Polish. According to Polish folklore, if a baby is born with teeth, and the baby suddenly dies, this baby will rise as a revenant (someone who's returned from the dead) and become an upior. The upior feeds on—surprise!—blood. To drink, the upior pierces the victim's skin and drains their blood with a sharp barb at the end of their tongue, usually between noon and midnight. After a long night of feeding, the upior will lean over their grave and up-chuck blood into their coffin—yeah, mega gross. When dealing with the supernatural, you definitely want to keep that poncho ready!

Upyr, Not Upior

Okay, I've got another story for you. Listen well . . .

On a dark and dreary night, a man is riding through a cemetery. As he rides, he spots a person wearing a red shirt and a sheepskin coat. The man stops his wagon and the stranger asks, "May I have a ride into the village?" The man agrees, but as the two head into the village, something feels . . . off.

The man notices that all the houses have crosses nailed to their gates. The passenger, observing that all the gates are locked, points to a home at the end of the road. There is no cross on the gate of that home, and when they reach it, the gate swings open by itself. The passenger disembarks and asks the man to accompany him inside.

They enter the home, and a boy and old man are sitting inside. The passenger grabs a bucket, placing it near the boy, and then stabs him in the neck! The man watches in horror as the boy's blood drains into the bucket. The passenger then turns to the old man and does the same thing. Once the buckets are filled with blood, he sits and drinks.

The man watches, frozen. Finally, the passenger says, "Come with me." As if in a trance, the man follows him, and suddenly, the two are back at the cemetery. When the man realizes where he is, he runs. The passenger chases him, but it's too late. The rooster crows for daylight, and the passenger—the upyr—vanishes.

The next day, the villagers find the bodies of the boy and the old man in their home, completely drained of their blood. The villagers head for the cemetery to hunt for the upyr. They discover the upyr in a grave filled with fresh blood. The villagers plunge a stake into the heart of upyr, finishing off the monster once and for all.

Spooky, right? The upyr (also known as an oupyr or uppyr) is a vampiric revenant from Russian folklore. Much like the classic vampire that we're familiar with, the upyr is known for draining the blood of its victims. According to Russian folklore, an upyr is created when a witch or a sorcerer dies. The upyr will attack the children in their family first and then move on to the other members of their family—no one is safe.

You might be thinking, "That's cool, but why are you telling us this?" First of all, I love telling a spooky story. Second, I wanted to show you how big and little differences across countries and cultures make for an exciting variety of supernatural legends. The upior and the upyr are just two of many bloodsucking, undead legends across Europe—and the world! (More on that in the next chapter.)

But as you can see from the stories of the upior and the upyr, there are some key traits that form a big part of the vampire legend we're familiar with—like blood sucking, undeath, and staking. So how did we get from these particular not-so-friendly connoisseurs of blood to, well, Count Dracula? To figure that out, we need a little historical context. Let's crank the dial on our time machine to the medieval ages! Be warned: it's going to get WEIRD.

THE BLOODY MIDDLE AGES

So, the Middle Ages. What were they in the middle of, anyway? Well, the Middle Ages took place between around 500 to 1500 CE. This thousand-year period in European history kicks off with the fall of the Roman Empire and ends with the start of the Renaissance. The Renaissance was considered a time of social change and of advances in art, philosophy, and culture. (And yes, the Teenage Mutant Ninja Turtles—Leonardo, Donatello, Michelangelo, and Raphael—are named after four famous Renaissance artists.)

During the Middle Ages, sometimes also called the Dark Ages, European people's daily lives were heavily influenced by religion and especially the Catholic Church. While there were artistic and agricultural advances, this period is known for the devastation of the Black Death, also called the bubonic plague. But before we get into how that relates to the vampire origin story, let's meet a famous medieval figure!

Interview with an Impaler

Vlad Tepes (a.k.a. Vlad III, a.k.a. Vlad the Impaler, a.k.a. Vlad Dracula) went down in history as a brutal figure known for impaling his enemies. But what made him just so terrifying? Well, we're in luck, dear reader! We were able to get answers from Vlad himself! You're probably thinking, "But isn't he dead?" Er, yes, technically. Never mind. Don't think about it too hard.

GUIDE: Thank you for being here with us, Vlad! Sorry to wake you from such a deep slumber for an interview, but we're happy you're here.

VLAD: Where am I? Who are you? What is this thing you're holding to my face?

GUIDE: It's a . . . microphone. On to the questions! Can you tell us where you were born, Vlad? And about your family?

VLAD: Oh. Certainly. I was born in 1431 in Transylvania. My father, Vlad II, ruled Wallachia with an iron fist. I was the second of four sons. My father took on the name Vlad Dracul after joining the Order of the Dragon, a military order—and that's why I was called Dracula, or "son of the dragon."

GUIDE: Great! So . . . about impaling heads on spikes, I have a couple of questions about why—

VLAD: My father took me and my brother Radu to a meeting ordered by Sultan Murad II. We were arrested, but my father was promised that he would survive if he left us behind. But he was tricked. Warlords killed my father and my brother Mircea—rest their souls.

GUIDE: I'm so sorry to hear that, but about the spiked heads . . . How did—

VLAD: I was raised by the Ottomans in captivity. They trained my brother and me to be fierce warriors. When I was set free from the Ottomans, I vowed my revenge! I thirsted for the blood of my enemies.

GUIDE: Oh, and there it is . . .

VLAD: My main goal, my only goal, was to obtain my father's throne and exact revenge on the Ottoman Empire once and for all. I defeated many enemies, even my brother Radu, who sided

with the Ottoman Empire—THE FOOL!

GUIDE: So, the heads . . .

VLAD: I gained my father's throne, going into battle for eight years to regain control of Wallachia. Once I was finally on the throne, I, Vlad the Impaler, did not stop until I ruled ALL! I killed over 80,000 people and put their heads on stakes so that everyone could see! I was a conqueror. A warrior. A KING!

GUIDE: Well, that's about all we have time for today! Thank you so much for telling us your history, Vlad. Oh, but one more question. Some say you're the inspiration for Bram Stoker's Count Dracula. Others have even claimed that you were a real-life vampire. What do you have to say about this?

VLAD: Who is this . . . Bram? Who is this Count Dracula? My name is VLAD DRACULA!

GUIDE: What you're saying is . . . you don't drink blood, change into a bat at night, or have a garlic allergy?

VLAD: *Garlic*? I laugh at garlic! I am VLAD DRACULA! Leader of men! Impaler of heads!

GUIDE: O-kay. I think I've heard enough. Go to sleep!

Whew, what a terrifying guy to interview! Again, please don't ask how we got him here! You may be wondering, "So, what does THIS have to do with Dracula? This dude just beheaded people!" You're right! Despite his bloodthirsty ways, Vlad wasn't a vampire. But scholars believe that Bram Stoker may have been inspired by Vlad's name when naming Count Dracula in the late 1800s.

The Plague

So how did vampires make it big? Let's look at history.

In 1347, the Black Death landed on European shores when twelve ships arrived in Messina, a port in Italy. When the ship docked, most of the crew aboard was found dead. The ones who made it out were mysteriously sick with . . . something. They complained of chills, body aches, diarrhea, and vomiting and began developing black spots on their skin. (This was the symptom that inspired the name Black Death.) Shortly after, this illness would spread quickly throughout Europe. Between 1347 and 1351, over 20 million people died from the bubonic plague (another name for the Black Death).

It turns out, the bacteria for this terrible plague was transmitted via fleas. But without a scientific explanation, some people at the time thought it was divine punishment from the heavens. Others sought out different explanations . . . and even blamed vampires!

According to Science

How did vaccines come to be? In the eighteenth century, smallpox hit Europe hard. Edward Jenner, an English doctor, wanted to help. He noticed that milkmaids who worked with cows with cowpox (an infection similar to smallpox) didn't catch smallpox. In 1796, Jenner tested this with James Phipps, whom he inoculated with pus from the cowpox blisters of milkmaid Sarah Nelmes—and James became immune to smallpox!

THE VAMPIRE PANIC OF THE 1700S

In the 1700s, disease ran rampant in Europe. Without medical advancements like vaccines or accurate knowledge of how diseases were transmitted, many people died from diseases like the plague, tuberculosis, and smallpox. Without any real way of understanding what was happening, some people started to come to one conclusion: vampires were running amok in Europe and causing disease!

Panic on the Streets of Serbia!

In 1725, a man from the Serbian village of Kisiljevo named Petar Blagojević died. End of story, right? Wrong. See, shortly after Petar died, nine other people mysteriously passed away. People in Kisiljevo started to talk. They claimed that they'd seen Petar walking around out of his grave. Rumors spread that Petar had brutally murdered his son and drunk his blood. Petar's wife even said that he showed up after he died, demanding his shoes.

The villagers and the town priest went to Petar's grave to dig up his body. They discovered that his corpse looked like he had never died. He had new skin and nails, his hair and beard had continued growing, and he had blood in his mouth—to the villagers, this was proof that he was a vampire! The villagers took a stake and plunged it into Petar's chest, hoping that this would get rid of their vampire problem once and for all.

Why did people believe Petar was a vampire? The answer lies in the science of decomposition!

Breaking Down Decomposition

When a human dies, their body starts decomposing within just a few minutes. But when you bury a corpse, the cold temperature of the ground slows decomposition. Back in Petar's day, people assumed that when a person dies, their body immediately rots. If you're dead, you're dead! So imagine being a regular villager in the 1700s. You open up a coffin, expecting to see a completely decomposed corpse, and it doesn't look any different. That would totally freak you out! Especially if you weren't sure what the cause of death was.

Another key fact is that when a corpse starts to decay, the body begins leaking blood out of its eyes, nose, mouth, and ears. People back in the 1700s who saw this concluded that it had to be the work of vampires. And of course, you know from Chapter 1 why hair and nails might appear to grow after death.

There were more cases like Petar's, including that of Arnold Paole, who died in Serbia in 1726 and was believed to have killed sixteen people—*after* he died. The Austrian government even sent a field surgeon named Johannes Flückinger to investigate. Europe was descending into full-blown vampire hysteria!

With vampire panic on the rise, people did what they could to combat the threat of any possible vampire attacks. Some took matters into their own hands and dug up the deceased to examine their corpses. Others tried different methods to keep the corpses down, including putting a heavy boulder on the corpse, placing a sickle around the corpse's neck, and shoving rocks into the corpse's mouth.

And as a last resort, they would stake and burn the corpse.

To us, vampires might be the subjects of spooky tales or the sparkly stars of a blockbuster movie. But to people living hundreds of years ago in Europe, vampires were how they made sense of the terrifying unknowns of plague and disease. Throughout history, the supernatural has often acted as both a reflection of our fears and the answer to our questions. Take a second to think: Do you have any questions about the world? Are you curious about what the answers to those questions are? How would you go about finding those answers?

Sorry, got distracted there with all those deep thoughts. Anyway, back to vampires. Stories of bloodsucking supernatural entities aren't unique to Europe. There are legends of different kinds of bloodsuckers all over the world! Grab your Fang-tactic Vampire Kit (see page 38) and follow me—in the next chapter, we're off on a globe-trotting adventure!

But first, let's do a little science . . .

Kitchen Decomposition

Decomposition might sound gross, but it's an important part of the cycle of life. Without decomposition, we'd have a lot of dead stuff on our hands! We need decomposition to break down organic matter and for new life to flourish. Without decomposition, we wouldn't have veggies, grains, or fruits. And without decomposers—such as worms and bacteria—we wouldn't have decomposition! So be kind to your friendly neighborhood decomposer.

Now's your chance to try out a little decomposition in your own kitchen with composting. Let's say you have an old piece of fruit or some apple peels. Instead of chucking it in the garbage, you can transform it into nutritious soil for your garden by helping it break down and decompose more quickly. Here's a simple way to get into composting.

First, gather your compostable materials:

WHAT TO COMPOST:
- Eggshells
- Dry leaves, twigs, sticks, grass, plants
- Fruit scraps
- Veggie scraps
- Cardboard, paper towels, napkins

WHAT NOT TO COMPOST:

- Dairy products (milk, cheese, eggs, yogurt)
- Meat and grease
- Animal poop
- Onion peels
- Orange or other citrus peels

You'll need a large plastic bin or a trash can with a lid, a drill to puncture holes (with adult supervision!), soil, shredded newspaper, and some water.

With your parent's or guardian's help, drill 10 large holes about 2 inches apart around the entirety of the bin until you get back to the first hole. After that, put the newspaper inside the bin, then the soil. Next, bury your compostable materials in the soil. Spray the top of the materials with water, and then put the lid on. Ta-da! You now have a compost bin. Here are some tips:

- Make sure to have a good mix of dry materials (like dry leaves, newspapers, etc.) and wet materials (like fruit and veggie scraps), with more dry than wet.
- Every five days, roll the bin around to keep everything mixed.

There's a wealth of information online about other ways to compost and how to level up your compost game. Definitely check it out if you're interested in reducing waste and creating delicious soil for your plant friends—and your decomposer friends! Happy composting!

Chapter 4

BLOODSUCKERS AROUND THE WORLD

We can't stop here, this is bat country!

—Hunter S. Thompson, *Fear and Loathing in Las Vegas*

We've covered some vampires from the European neck of the woods, but there are plenty more supernatural bloodsuckers from all over the world! They may not be vampires, but they share a lot in common with vampires: they love blood and they love a good shapeshifting moment. Let's take a spin around the globe! I'm going to introduce you to a few new monsters from myth, legend, and folklore. It's a big world, after all . . .

HELLO my name is:

Jiangshi

Jiangshi (殭屍 in Chinese), like vampires, are undead beings. Unlike vampires, the jiangshi craves your life force (known as qi), not your blood. Also called the Chinese hopping vampire or Chinese hopping zombie, the jiangshi goes by different names in different Asian cultures, like vampir cina in Indonesia and cường thi in Vietnamese.

ORIGIN: China

APPEARANCE: A hopping corpse with arms outstretched. Often portrayed in traditional Qing dynasty clothes with a paper talisman (a.k.a. an item with special powers that imparts good luck, protection, or healing) stuck to their head.

BACKSTORY: The primary explanation for the jiangshi legend has its roots in old burial traditions. It was believed that if someone passed away and was buried far from their home, their soul would grow homesick. To prevent this, families would pay for their deceased one to be transported home. One method of transport was to pay a priest to conduct a ritual to reanimate the corpse and have the corpse hop all the way home. In practice, this meant the corpses were tied to bamboo rods carried by two men. From far away, this made the corpses look like they were hopping up and down the road—a terrifying sight! Want to see a jiangshi? There's actually a whole film genre inspired by them. Famous Hong Kong films within the jiangshi genre are *Encounters of the Spooky Kind*, *Mr. Vampire*, and *The Era of Vampires*.

LIKES: Hometowns, hopping, delicious qi of the living

DISLIKES: Mirrors, vinegar, fire, jujube seeds, glutinous rice, red beans, brooms, talismans, having to bend their knees or arms

HELLO my name is:

Chupacabra

The chupacabra, a word that means "goat sucker" in Spanish, is a creature that feeds on animals such as sheep, goats, and even coyotes. Chupacabra sightings have been reported in Texas, Puerto Rico, Mexico, and other places.

ORIGIN: Puerto Rico

APPEARANCE: Accounts vary! The chupacabra can look reptile-like or dog-like, with glowing red eyes and short forelimbs.

BACKSTORY: In the 1990s, there were reports of attacks on livestock in Puerto Rico. Farmers found their animals drained of blood and left with puncture wounds. This, to these farmers and many others, was the work of what would become known as the chupacabra! Soon, more incidents followed in other countries, including Mexico, Brazil, Chile, Colombia, El Salvador, Nicaragua, Panama, the Dominican Republic, Bolivia, and Peru.

LIKES: Feeding on delicious livestock (goats, sheep, cows, chickens, etc.), confusing farmers, causing problems on purpose

DISLIKES: Being hungry, probably

HELLO my name is:

Adze

The adze appear as fireflies. They feed on the blood of any human, but they particularly love the blood of babies or children.

ORIGIN: Togo and Ghana

APPEARANCE: A firefly! Or a person.

BACKSTORY: Adze appear in the folklore of the Ewe people, who live mainly in southern Togo and Ghana. In their firefly form, the adze can flit through small spaces, such as keyholes, to get to their victims. Some historians think that adze folklore may be connected to malaria, a disease spread by mosquitoes. The adze might have served as a way of warning against this terrible disease and its carriers.

LIKES: Coconut water or milk, palm oil, blood, keyholes, small gaps

DISLIKES: Firefly catchers

HELLO my name is:

Soucouyant

According to folklore, soucouyants (also known as Heg, Soucouyen, Soukoyan, Aseme, and Ol'Higue) are shapeshifters with a taste for blood.

ORIGIN: Trinidad and Tobago, Dominica, Guadeloupe, Guyana, Haiti, Grenada, Belize, Jamaica, Barbados, the Bahamas, Saint Lucia, and the state of Louisiana

APPEARANCE: Can appear as an elderly woman by day and a beautiful young woman or a fireball at night.

BACKSTORY: The soucouyant appears in a variety of legends and folklore, particularly Caribbean folklore. What the soucouyant is most known for is shedding her skin at night and transforming into a fireball that resembles a corpse candle. (A corpse candle is a small flame that is considered an omen of someone's impending death.) During the nighttime, the soucouyant comes out to prey on sleeping victims, particularly men. When she attacks, she leaves two small bite marks on her victim's body. The person who is attacked by the soucouyant will either die from being drained of blood or turn into a soucouyant themselves. One way to stop a soucouyant is to sprinkle rice along your doorway. When the soucouyant sees the rice on the floor, they'll immediately bend down to count the grains of rice, giving you a chance to escape!

LIKES: Sleeping people, black magic, small spaces, shedding skin and storing it in a mortar

---

DISLIKES: Sticks, scattered rice, seasoning—especially salt, garlic, and hot pepper

HELLO my name is:

Aswang

Aswang can refer to different supernatural beings in Filipino folklore, but we're talking about the vampire variety of aswang. During the day, aswangs can look just like you or me, but at night, it's a whole different story!

ORIGIN: Philippines

APPEARANCE: It depends on the aswang!

BACKSTORY: Within Filipino folklore, the aswang includes a variety of evil shapeshifters—some of whom can even blend in with regular humans. There are many different types of aswang, but let's talk about two that have a thirst for blood: Tik-tiks take their name from the owl that flies along with them when they hunt their sleeping prey. The owl makes a *tik-tik* noise. This aswang can appear as a regular human during the day, doing all the regular things that we do, but at night the aswang transforms into a bird and uses their long tongue to pierce a hole into their victim for a little bloodsucking. Once they're done, they go back home to feed their babies with the blood they've stored up.

Another type of aswang is a shapeshifter that can transform into a beautiful person but usually resembles an old woman with black hair, a long black tongue, and bloodshot eyes. When this shapeshifter looks for prey, they typically go after women, children, and people who are ill. They create a replica of their victim using sticks and grass and banana leaves, and this replica goes running around. Why? Because while the replica is out in the world, the shapeshifter takes the actual victim to their lair to feed. Yikes!

LIKES: Meat, meat, and more meat—blood, flesh, mucus, organs, you name it! Also, sipping blood through a tongue straw and blending in with humans.

DISLIKES: Garlic, ash, salt, ginger, religious items and amulets, urine

HELLO my name is:

Langsuir

In Malaysian mythology, the langsuir (or langsuyar) is the ghost, or revenant, of a woman who has died during childbirth.

ORIGIN: Malaysia

APPEARANCE: A tall, beautiful woman with red eyes, long black hair, and long fingernails wearing a green robe . . . or a woman's head connected to her spine and entrails.

BACKSTORY: According to legend, the langsuir are women who passed away during childbirth and rose again with a thirst for blood. One version of the langsuir has a hole in the back of her neck through which she drinks blood—no fangs involved. The langsuir is also said to be able to fly and, in some legends, can even transform into an owl. If a langsuir is caught and the hole in her neck filled with her hair, she transforms into a beautiful human woman. As for their prey, the langsuir feeds on humans, particularly newborn babies.

LIKES: Flying through the night sky, owls, snacking on fish

DISLIKES: Haircuts, manicures, glass beads in their mouth, needles in their hands, eggs under their armpits

According to Science

While not a supernatural creature, the vampire bat is one of the coolest little dudes on the planet. As mentioned in Chapter 1, the vampire bat is hematophagous. Unlike other kinds of bats, they feed exclusively on blood—nothing else. They sleep during the day, hanging out in total darkness with their batty crew until it's time to hunt. They eat every two days and share food with their fellow vampire bats to survive. To feed, they sink their teeth into their prey, such as pigs, birds, cows, or horses, and start drinking—but it doesn't hurt their prey or even wake them up. And don't worry: vampire bats don't usually feed on humans, though there have been reports of bats feeding on people in parts of Brazil. In general, bats are best appreciated from a distance. Their bite, accidental or not, can result in rabies.

And there you have it—just a few of the many bloodsuckers around the world. I could use a little break from all that traveling. How about we kick back with a good book? What's that? You didn't pack one? Well, lucky for you, my friend, I brought along plenty of spooky reads. Let's say our goodbyes to bat country and dive into some fang-tastic literature.

Chapter 5

READ IT AND SCREAM

Listen to them,
the children of the night.
What music they make!

—Count Dracula,
Dracula

Now that we've met bloodsuckers from all around the world, it's time we got to know THE most famous bloodsucker of all: Dracula! We're going to crack open a few classics and venture into the terrifying pages of vampire literature— where the shadows are long and the tales are tall. Let this chapter of the Read It and Scream Book Club come to order! And yes, there will be spoilers.

VAMPIRE LIT IS . . . LIT!

Vampires have appeared in legends and myths since ancient times, and as you learned, they took center stage when mysterious plagues devastated Europe. Before vampires swooped into literature, they popped up in reports and works of nonfiction.

Remember Petar Blagojević and Arnold Paole? When vampire panic was at its peak in the 1700s, the Austrian government documented its vampire investigations. And back in 1689, Johann Weikhard Freiherr von Valvasor released a report about vampires in a fifteen-volume encyclopedia titled *The Glory of the Duchy of Carniola*. This report detailed the vampire beliefs and practices that he studied in Eastern

Europe. It wasn't until 1748 that Heinrich August Ossenfelder published a poem titled *Der Vampir*, or *The Vampire*, which tells the tale of a man attempting to seduce a young woman toward the dark side (not the Star Wars kind—the vampire kind). And in 1819, the first work of vampire literature burst out of the grave.

Read All About It

Vampires have been written into just about every genre of fiction—romance, sci-fi, fantasy, you name it. But horror, specifically gothic horror, is where vampires reign supreme! Gothic horror (or gothic fiction) tends to be a haunting story that features the supernatural in some way, along with a bleak or tragic setting that sends shivers down your spine. Named after the Gothic-style architecture that appeared in some of the first gothic novels, gothic fiction began in the late eighteenth century with *The Castle of Otranto* by Horace Walpole. Other gothic novels include *The Strange Case of Dr. Jekyll and Mr. Hyde* by Robert Louis Stevenson, *Wuthering Heights* by Emily Brontë, *Beloved* by Toni Morrison, *The Picture of Dorian Gray* by Oscar Wilde, *The Mysteries of Udolpho* by Ann Radcliffe, and just about everything by Edgar Allan Poe!

IT WAS A DARK AND STORMY NIGHT . . .

During the summer of 1816, English poet Lord Byron invited a couple of friends to his mansion in Switzerland. The guest list included fellow writers Mary Wollstonecraft Shelley and her husband, Percy Bysshe Shelley, and Lord Byron's physician, Dr. John Polidori. The days were dark and dreary, and everyone was stuck inside. To pass the time, Byron proposed a challenge: write a scary story! Mary Shelley ended up writing *Frankenstein, or the Modern Prometheus* (sound familiar?), and Dr. John Polidori created the short story "The Vampyre: A Tale"—the granddaddy of vampire fiction!

Vampyre with a Y

So, what's the deal with "The Vampyre"? Let me get out my handy dandy notes and tell you. Where . . . Ah! Here they are! Polidori's story goes like this:

Lord Ruthven, a charming and mysterious nobleman, goes on a road trip around Europe with Aubrey, a young man he met in London. But what Aubrey doesn't know is that Lord Ruthven is (drumroll, please) secretly a vampire! Aubrey eventually splits with Lord Ruthven and along the way, Aubrey falls in love with Ianthe, an innkeeper's daughter.

But life says "nope" to Aubrey, and his girlfriend is found dead. Her throat had been mysteriously ripped apart. And coincidentally, Ianthe's murder happens right after Lord Ruthven visits her village. Aubrey doesn't suspect a thing (*seriously?*), and the two become besties again. When Lord Ruthven is mortally wounded in a fight with bandits, he makes Aubrey promise not to talk about him, or his death, for a year and a day. Yeah, it's very, very suspicious.

Of course, as you've probably figured out, Lord Ruthven isn't really dead. He comes back, good as new, and gets engaged to Aubrey's sister . . . and their wedding is on the day Aubrey's promise to Lord Ruthven expires! Bound by his oath, Aubrey can't say a word but writes a letter to warn his sister. Tragically, Aubrey dies and the letter doesn't make it to his sister in time. Lord Ruthven marries Aubrey's sister and vanishes on their wedding night, leaving Aubrey's sister drained of her blood. (Pro-tip: When your sister is about to be eaten by your ex-best friend who's a VAMPIRE SERIAL KILLER, break your oath! Tell her immediately!)

Dr. Polidori was said to have modeled Lord Ruthven after his charismatic host, Lord Byron. Lord Ruthven wasn't like the scary, bloodthirsty vampires in folklore. No, he was charming, friendly, and romantic—but definitely still mega-evil. "The Vampyre" introduced the world to a new kind of vampire.

THE PENNY DREADFUL!

Thanks to increased literacy and technological advances, demand for fiction shot up in the 1800s, and penny dreadfuls answered the call. These were thrilling works of fiction, which were released in short installments every week, sold for a penny. Regular, working-class people could afford them; reading wasn't just for the wealthy anymore. These stories were exciting and fast reads, featuring murder, the supernatural, and plenty of drama. Ever heard of Sweeney Todd, the demon barber? He first appeared in the penny dreadful *The String of Pearls*.

In the 1840s, James Malcolm Rymer and Thomas Peckett Prest published *Varney the Vampire*. It was initially released as a penny dreadful and told the story of Sir Francis Varney, who targets a wealthy family for their money and their blood. *Varney the Vampire* introduced details like vampires having sharp fangs and powers of hypnosis, which influenced vampire fiction for years to come.

And now that you know a little more about the history of vampire lit, let's meet the very first lady vampire in vampire literature, Carmilla!

OUR LADY OF FANGS, CARMILLA

Published in 1872 by Irish author Joseph Sheridan La Fanu (twenty-five years before Dracula!), *Carmilla* is a novella (a very short novel) that featured the first female—and queer—vampire in fiction. What's it about? Let's sink our fangs into this story and find out . . .

So this kid Laura and her dad live in a small village in Austria, and even though she has a comfortable life, she still feels lonely. They await the arrival of a family friend named General Spielsdorf and his niece, Bertha, but they get a letter with horrible news: Bertha has died of a mysterious illness. One day, Laura remembers some strange dreams she used to have about a mysterious girl visiting her bedchamber.

Years later, when Laura is a teen, a carriage accident happens outside her home. Inside the carriage is a girl named Carmilla and her mother. And get this—when Laura sees Carmilla, she immediately recognizes her as the girl from her dreams! Carmilla's mom asks Laura's father to keep Carmilla with them for three months because she has to continue on her trip. (Totally not suspicious at all!) Laura and Carmilla become instant BFFs, but then, weird things start to happen: young women in the nearby village start mysteriously dying.

Later, Laura finds an old portrait from 1698, and she notices the woman in the painting looks just like Carmilla . . . but her name is actually Mircalla, Countess of Karnstein. Carmilla claims that the woman definitely isn't her, even though they look identical. Laura basically says, "okay, cool, you're acting real suspicious, but whatever," and moves on. Carmilla then takes Laura on a romantic, moonlit walk and tells her that she cares for her as more than a friend.

Soon after, Laura begins to grow sick. One night, she wakes to see a large black cat at the foot of her bed. Another night, she dreams that her deceased mother is warning her of danger, and then she dreams that Carmilla came into her room covered in blood.

Ye Olde History

During the Middle Ages, cats, especially black cats, were thought to be evil and associated with witchcraft and vampirism! Unfortunately, the stigma around black cats persists to this day. If you ever find yourself thinking about adopting a cat, consider a black cat—they make great pets, just like any other cat!

Eventually, Laura and her father go to visit General Spielsdorf, who is still grieving his niece, Bertha. He tells them about how Bertha and a mysterious woman named Mircalla became close friends, and soon after, Bertha became ill and died. You guessed it—Mircalla had been a vampire all along! When the general finally lays eyes on Carmilla, he leaps into action and tries to attack her. Carmilla escapes, and the general explains that the names Mircalla and Carmilla are anagrams of each other. Plot twist: the two women are one and the same!

Laura's father, the general, and a baron track down Carmilla's tomb and open it. They discover Carmilla lying in a blood-soaked grave. The men drive a stake through the vampire's heart, ending her undead life. Though free from her mysterious illness, Laura is saddened by the loss of her friend. But when she travels to Italy, she feels that Carmilla is right there with her—both the monster she knew her to be and the companion that she was.

And that's the story of Carmilla! In the past, this haunting novella was overshadowed by Bram Stoker's *Dracula*. However, these days, *Carmilla* is more popular than ever, inspiring novels and TV shows and even a web series on YouTube.

Ye Olde History

Bloodletting was a common practice that started in ancient Egypt. Doctors believed that some illnesses could be cured via bloodletting. One method of bloodletting was to use leeches! Leeches are a type of worm that are hematophagous, like vampire bats—they suck blood. Bloodletting as it was practiced in medieval times isn't considered safe to do anymore, medically speaking.

The One and Only Count Dracula

Ladies, gentlemen, and intrepid readers, it's the moment you've all been waiting for. Meet the writer of *Dracula* himself . . . Give it up for Bram Stoker!

GUIDE: Thank you so much for joining us, Bram! I'm a huge fan of your work! Can I get your autograph? You can sign my garlic bread.

BRAM STOKER: Excuse me, but who are you? How did I get here? Why am I covered in grave dirt? Why are those candles in a circle? And what is that nightmarish rectangular device you're holding? Does it contain demons?

GUIDE: It's a smartphone. Don't worry about it. Bram, our readers are dying to know more about you! Tell us about your life.

BRAM: Oh, well. That I can do. I was born in the seaside neighborhood of Clontarf, outside Dublin, Ireland, in 1847. When I was a young boy, I came down with a dreadful illness. To treat my illness, I was subject to bloodletting by my doctors. My mother, bless her soul, would tell me stories of terrible diseases and illnesses that she and others survived, and old folk tales as well.

GUIDE: Fascinating! What happened when you grew up?

BRAM: I had a passionate love for theater. A performance of *Hamlet*, in particular, captured my heart. I wrote a letter reviewing the performance and the letter landed in the hands of Henry Irving, an actor and owner of London's Lyceum Theater. He wrote back to me, asking if I wanted to manage the theater for him. I was thrilled! I married my wife, Florence Balcombe, and we set off to London.

GUIDE: And your boss, Henry Irving, was one of your inspirations for Count Dracula?

BRAM: Correct. How did you—

GUIDE: Oh, just a lucky guess! So when did you start writing *Dracula*?

BRAM: Well, I started the manuscript for *Dracula* while working at the theater. I drew from several sources of inspiration: my tyrannical yet charming boss, Irving, the infamous serial killer Jack the Ripper, the tale of the Croglin Grange vampire in Cumberland, and Vlad the Impaler.

GUIDE: So, about your book. Give us the Sparknotes summary.

BRAM: The what now?

GUIDE: The short version. The 411. The hot goss. The piping hot tea.

BRAM: Do you always speak in tongues? Never mind. Well, my novel begins with a young lawyer named Jonathan Harker traveling to Transylvania to oversee the final stages of a real estate deal. As Harker approaches the home, there are wolves howling in the night, and the castle is surrounded by a terrible darkness. He meets the owner of the castle, a thin, pale man named Count Dracula.

GUIDE: Doesn't he go for Harker's neck almost immediately?

BRAM: Ah, you've read my work, I see. Yes, the count lunges at him but restrains himself. Later, Harker is set upon by three vampire women who try to eat him, but Dracula saves him. Harker then discovers the count's secret—he drinks the blood of the living! But before Harker can kill the count and escape the castle, Dracula leaves for England in search of more victims.

GUIDE: He leaves in boxes of dirt from Transylvania, right? Sounds uncomfortable.

BRAM: A vampire needs the dirt of his homeland, you know. So Mina Murray, Jonathan Harker's fiancée, travels to see her friend Lucy in a seaside town. There, they encounter a shipwreck with a dead captain, boxes of dirt, and a missing crew. After that terrifying incident, Lucy falls mysteriously ill. One night, Mina awakens to find that Lucy has wandered out to a graveyard. But Lucy has no memory of this and two puncture wounds on her neck.

GUIDE: Uh oh . . .

BRAM: Jonathan Harker, miraculously, makes it to Budapest. Mina leaves Lucy in the care of one of her three suitors, Dr. Seward. But as Lucy's condition worsens, they call in an expert, Van Helsing—a professor who specializes in vampires. Van Helsing immediately orders blood transfusions and has her room covered in garlic. She starts to recover, but then one night, as Lucy is resting, a wolf comes through the window and attacks her.

GUIDE: No! Not Lucy!

BRAM: After the attack, Lucy opens her mouth to reveal that her canine teeth have grown into long, sharp fangs. She tries to take a bite out of her fiancé, before passing away. But that isn't the end of her. Soon there are reports of a woman attacking in the night and trying to eat children. Van Helsing tells Lucy's suitors that Lucy now belongs to the "un-dead" and that they have to stop her before she strikes again. Together, they stake her heart and stuff her head with garlic.

GUIDE: One down, one to go . . . Dracula.

BRAM: Yes, but then Mina starts to take a turn for the worse. One night, Van Helsing and Dr. Seward find Harker unconscious and Mina . . . with Dracula!

GUIDE: He's back!

BRAM: Dracula has forced Mina to drink his blood from an open gash along his chest. The count disappears into the night before he can be captured. To track Dracula down, Van Helsing uses hypnosis on Mina to uncover Dracula's location via their psychic link and realizes he's headed to Transylvania! The men follow Dracula to Transylvania, fighting off Dracula's companions to get to the box with Count Dracula in it. One of Lucy's suitors takes a knife and plunges it into the count's heart, while Harker deals the final blow and cuts off the count's head.

GUIDE: And that's the end of *Dracula*! Did you know that there have been books, movies, and music inspired by your story?

BRAM: Fascinating. What are . . . movies?

GUIDE: Um, well, they're kind of like electronic theater that you can watch again and again.

BRAM: What's electronic . . . Never mind. Who plays Dracula? Is it my man Henry Irving?

GUIDE: No, it's a gentleman named Bela Lugosi. We'll talk about him in the next chapter. Anyway, thank you for chatting with me, Bram. Back behind the mortal veil you go!

Read All About It

Dracula is an epistolary novel, a.k.a. a story told through a series of documents, such as letters, newspaper clippings, journal entries, etc. For example, if you wrote a bunch of emails telling a long story about a werewolf who loves ice cream, that would be an epistolary novel! This style of writing lends a sense of realism to the story—it makes the reader feel like they're right there as things are happening. The story of Dracula is told through letters, diary entries, and journal entries. Here are a few other books written in the epistolary style: *Diary of a Wimpy Kid* by Jeff Kinney, *The Princess Diaries* by Meg Cabot, *Harriet the Spy* by Louise Fitzhugh, *the* Dork Diaries series by Rachel Renée Russell, and *The Vanderbeekers of 141st Street* by Karina Yan Glaser.

DRACULA OVER THE YEARS

Dracula changed the game for all the fictional vampires that followed. His ability to turn his victims into vampires instead of killing them, among many other abilities, shaped vampire lore for decades to come. And his story sparked many characters in later books, TV shows, and movies, such as Count von Count in *Sesame Street*, Count Dracula in *Hotel Transylvania*, Lord Dracula in *The Grim Adventures of Billy and Mandy*, and Dracula in *Castlevania*!

You've met Dracula, the blueprint for classic vampire fiction. In Chapter 6, we'll head to Hollywood to meet some modern vampires.

Build Your Own Scare

Have you ever wanted to write your very own spooky tale? Fill in the blanks below to create your own bloodcurdling, spine-chilling vampire story.

Listen carefully, _____, your life depends on it.
name 1

Every night, as the sun sets and the moon rises in the darkening sky, I look out my window and see this creature, this terrible _____ _____. It doesn't make a move to come
adjective   animal

inside my _____, but it's always crouching
place

beneath the _____, silently watching. One night, it
noun

_____, and I watched in horror as it began to creep
past-tense verb

past the _____ _____ in my yard. I heard the scrabble
color   noun

of sharp claws against the back door and a haunting cry that

sounded like a _____.
creature

When I looked out the window again, I glimpsed a shadowy figure and the burning red embers of two eyes watching me, always watching me. This creature of the night wore a sweeping black cape and a _____. I felt _____ as our
noun   emotion

eyes locked. Then the figure disappeared. When I awoke the

following day, I stumbled to my kitchen and poured myself a

bowl of _____. As I checked my texts, I learned that
           food

my friend _____ from _____ had fallen
           name 2   town name

strangely ill after seeing this same being. _____ sent me a
                                             He/she/they

photo of twin puncture wounds on _____ neck.
                                 his/her/their

It is night again, and I am afraid. The wispy, moonlit clouds re-

semble a _____. I see a shadow approaching my door, and
         noun

I feel a curious compulsion to _____ and open the door.
                               verb

I can sense my blood pumping through my veins, the roar of

my heartbeat in my ears. I smell the scent of _____ in
                                              plural noun

the air. I want to _____ or _____, but it's too
                   verb   verb

late. _____ has fallen prey to this vampire . . . and I fear
      Name 2

that I may be next.

Chapter 6

LIGHTS, CAMERA, VAMPIRES

Nick: Twilight!

Deacon: Shut up, Nick!
You are not Twilight.

—*What We Do in
the Shadows* (2014)

Welcome to Hollywood! Grab your popcorn, take a seat, and direct your eyeballs and earballs to the silver screen. You may be asking yourself, "Oh super wise and incredibly cool guide person, have vampires really changed that much from classic literature to modern-day media?" Yes, yes, and yes, dear reader. Dim the lights and raise the curtain. The show's about to begin! (Don't worry, there'll be an intermission for snacks and bathroom breaks.)

ACT 1: *NOSFERATU*

If we're diving deep into vampire cinema, we have to talk about one of the first vampire films to put bloodsuckers on the map! Directed by F. W. Murnau, the silent film *Nosferatu* was a force to be reckoned with when it hit German screens in 1922. The film was an adaptation of Bram Stoker's *Dracula*, but there were a few key differences.

Nosferatu's Count Orlok, whom we met in Chapter 1, was the complete opposite of Count Dracula! With his spooky appearance and haunting demeanor, Count Orlok was the stuff of nightmares. Not only that, in the novel, Count Dracula isn't seriously hurt by the sunlight. But Count Orlok is the first major vampire in the media that we see killed by sunlight shining directly on him. And fun fact: Count Orlok was played by Max Schreck, a German actor many believed was a vampire himself—his acting was that convincing!

According to Science

"Blood is life!" as Knock said in the film *Nosferatu*. But, like, what *is* it? Blood is made up of blood cells (white cells, red cells, and platelets) and plasma (a liquid containing nutrients, proteins, and hormones that blood cells float around in). Blood transports oxygen and nutrients around our body via the circulatory system. The average human contains up to 1.2 to 1.5 gallons of blood. That's about 5 liters, or around 7 percent to 10 percent of your body weight! If you're old enough and meet the qualifications (like having enough iron), you can donate blood to other people who need it. And just FYI, the blue whale has 1,165 gallons (5,300 liters) of blood, an elephant has up to 65 gallons (245 liters), and a cow has 10 gallons (38 liters)!

ACT 2: *DRACULA*, THE MOVIE

It's the year 1931, almost ten years after *Nosferatu* hit theaters. Universal Studios really, really wanted to bring Dracula to the silver screen and paid $40,000 for the film and stage rights to *Dracula*. But there was just one problem: who would play the role of Count Dracula?

Hungarian actor Bela Lugosi, that's who. Lugosi wasn't a stranger to the role of Dracula—he'd portrayed the count many times in plays and was the perfect fit.

The Vampire Will Be Televised

When Bela Lugosi died, his wife and son requested that he be buried in the iconic Dracula costume! However, the cape that he wore was a replica. He left the original cape with his son. In 2011, the cape was up for auction for more than $1 million, but it failed to go to the highest bidder. Instead, the family decided to donate it to the Academy Museum of Motion Pictures, and that's where it lives today!

When *Dracula* opened in New York in 1931, audiences were hooked. Bela Lugosi commanded the screen, giving a mesmerizing and memorable performance as Count Dracula that stuck with viewers for years to come. In time, Dracula became a classic movie monster right up there with Frankenstein's monster. But soon, filmmakers and movie studios were itching to release something new, something no one had ever seen before.

INTERMISSION: AN EPIDEMIC OF VAMPIRES

Stretch your legs and grab more snacks! We're at our first intermission break. While we're here, let me tell you about the virus variety of vampire. The two films that started the virus vampire movement are *The Last Man on Earth* (1964) and *The Omega Man* (1971), both of which are based on the novel *I Am Legend* by Richard Matheson. These movies feature ordinary people turned into vampires thanks to a science-based or manufactured virus. Now, you might be thinking, "That's just like zombies!" Well, you're right! These vampires share a lot of similarities with zombies. Let's compare the two (opposite).

ZOMBIES	VIRUS VAMPIRES
Start out as regular humans	Start out as regular humans
Eat brains	Drink blood
Shuffle at three speeds: slow, fast, and super fast	Move fast—faster than regular vampires
Skin is decaying and sometimes gray	Discolored skin with prominent and protruding veins
Eyes can stay normal, turn white, or be bloodshot	Eye color change is common, with shades including gold or amber
Contagious bite will turn you into a zombie	Contagious bite will turn you into a vampire

Back in Chapter 3, you read about how people in the past blamed vampires for the plagues going around Europe. It's all connected! The virus subgenre of vampire films feeds into that fear of contagious disease and the unexplainable, leading to films telling stories about vampire plagues, such as the movie *Daybreakers* (2009) and the modern adaptation of *I Am Legend* (2007).

Heads up—the show is about to start again! Got your snacks? Good. On with the show!

ACT 3: THE AGE OF TELEVISION

After the massive success of vampires on the silver screen, television was the next stop! Vampires appeared on popular TV shows like *The Addams Family* and *Dark Shadows*. But it was a certain chosen one who stuck television with the pointy end.

The Vampire Will Be Televised

By the 1980s and 1990s, a new kind of vampire emerged in film. Movies like *Fright Night* (1985), *My Best Friend Is a Vampire* (1987), and *Vamp* (1986) showed the campy, comedic side of vampires, while films like *Near Dark* (1987) and *The Lost Boys* (1987) portrayed the gritty underbelly of the vampire world.

Into Every Generation a Slayer Is Born . . .

Premiering in 1997, the show *Buffy the Vampire Slayer* centered around Buffy, a girl who was the latest in the line of slayers, young women with mystical powers who are tasked with fighting supernatural creatures like vampires and demons. The show was a runaway hit! Like *Dracula*, *Buffy the Vampire Slayer* gave us a whole new take on vampires and vampire hunters. In this show, slayers possessed some of the physical abilities that vampires had, like strength, agility, and stamina, and they wielded "Mister Pointy," a sharp stake that halted vampires in their tracks.

There's a lot to enjoy about iconic vampire TV, but one common element you'll see in some of the biggest shows is the vampire love triangle. For Buffy, her two vampire admirers are Spike and Angel. In *The Vampire Diaries*, Elena has vampires Stefan and Damon vying for her hand, while in *True Blood*, Sookie must choose between Bill and Eric. But there's one particular love triangle that took the vampire fandom (or fangdom) by storm . . . yes, I'm talking about *Twilight*.

From Tomb to Screen

In addition to *Buffy*, *True Blood*, and *The Vampire Diaries*, there are plenty of other vampire shows out there. Here are a few recent ones:

- ● **What We Do in the Shadows (2019):** This mockumentary-style show (based on the 2014 movie of the same name) centers around the daily lives of a group of vampire roommates who have been together for centuries.

- *A Discovery of Witches* (2018): Based on the All Souls book series by Deborah Harkness, this fantasy features Diana, a witch, and Matthew, a vampire, as they work together to protect a mysterious and powerful book.
- *First Kill* (2022): This supernatural show based on author V. E. Schwab's short story follows a vampire hunter named Calliope and a vampire named Juliette.

How about movies? The novels *Dracula* and *I Am Legend* have had fang-tastic book-to-screen adaptations (or as I like to call them, vampdaptations) over the years. Some other vampire movies and the books that inspired them include:

- *Interview with the Vampire* (1994), inspired by *Interview with the Vampire* by Anne Rice
- *Blade* (1998), inspired by the comic *Blade* created by Marv Wolfman (writer) and Gene Colan (artist)
- *Let the Right One In* (2008), inspired by *Let the Right One In* by John Ajvide Lindqvist
- *Vampire Academy* (2014), inspired by the Vampire Academy series by Richelle Mead
- *Abraham Lincoln: Vampire Hunter* (2012), inspired by *Abraham Lincoln: Vampire Hunter* by Seth Grahame-Smith

Supernaturalist Scavenger Hunt

While this book is a great starting point for your supernatural journey, there's so much more to discover. To get you started, try out this scavenger hunt at your local library. And if you need help finding a book, ask your librarian. Librarians are awesome! I'm a fan.

CAN YOU FIND THESE BOOKS?

1. A book about a bunny with fangs: _____

2. A book in which vampires wear polka dots: _____

3. A book about a small vampire: _____

4. A picture book about a family of vampires taking a trip to the zoo: _____

5. A series with the word *Fang* in the title: _____

6. A book about a pig who slays vampires: _____

7. A picture book about fangs: _____

8. A book about a vampire slayer: _____

9. A book written by Bram Stoker: _____

10. A nonfiction guide to the supernatural: _____

ANSWER KEY:

Before we get into the answers, a quick note—some of these questions have multiple answers, and you might have found a different book. There is a wealth of vampire books out there, after all!

1. *Bunnicula* by Deborah and James Howe

2. *Vampires Don't Wear Polka Dots* by Marcia Jones & Debbie Dadey

3. *The Little Vampire* by Angela Sommer-Bodenburg

4. *Vampenguin* by Lucy Ruth Cummins

5. The Amelia Fang series by Laura Ellen Anderson

6. *Ham Helsing* by Rich Moyer

7. *I Love My Fangs!* by Kelly Leigh Miller

8. *Buffy the Vampire Slayer: New School Nightmare* by Casey Nowak

9. *Dracula* by (say it with me) Bram Stoker

10. *Hanging with Vampires: A Totally Factual Field Guide to the Supernatural* a.k.a. this guide!

So how did you do on this scavenger hunt? Now that you have a stack of vampire books on your hands, are you planning to read any of them?

ACT 4: SHINE BRIGHT LIKE A VAMPIRE

Young adult literature, or YA lit, has been home to many a vampire tale. YA vampire lit features storylines centering friendship, romance, surviving high school, and the eternal struggle of becoming an immortal vampire, among other things. Some examples include *Blue Bloods* by Melissa de la Cruz, *Vampire Kisses* by Ellen Schreiber, and *Vampire Academy* by Richelle Mead.

In 2005, the YA novel *Twilight* by Stephenie Meyer landed in bookstores, and everyone drank it up like, well, vampires drinking blood! *Twilight* tells the story of a teenage girl named Bella Swan. She moves to the foggy town of Forks, Washington, with her father and falls in love with Edward Cullen, who is incredibly handsome and also (surprise!) a 104-year-old vampire. A few things complicate Bella's epic love story with Edward: rivalries with other vampires and werewolves, a love triangle (Team Edward! No, Team Jacob!), and, of course, the fact that Bella is a human and Edward is a vampire. Since the first book in the series was published, over 100 million copies of the Twilight books have sold worldwide.

Beginning in 2008, the Twilight series was adapted into movies, which were also massively popular, raking in over 3.4 billion dollars. The Twilight franchise was known for its swoon-worthy romance and, of course, Edward Cullen, the sparkly and handsome vampire. Yeah, a pretty big departure from the terrifying bloodsucking legends of the past! But in a way, Edward isn't so different from his vampiric predecessors like the charming Lord Ruthven and Count Dracula. Audiences have been drawn to stories of terrifying and alluring vampires for centuries.

But Wait, We Have to Talk About . . .

Critics of the Twilight series have wrestled with a number of issues; Bella and Edward's relationship isn't exactly healthy, for one thing. Critics have also pointed out the sexism in Twilight and the lack of—and deeply flawed—representation. In the movies, the character of Laurent, played by Edi Gathegi, is the only Black vampire. And within the books, the culture of the Quileute Tribe, a Native American tribe in La Push, Washington, is used and misrepresented. To make matters worse, despite Twilight's stunning financial success at the box office and the bookstore, the Quileute Tribe didn't profit or benefit from the use of their culture and land.

Critiques like these are incredibly important and raise crucial questions about diversity and inclusion in film and fiction. How do we ensure that art has a positive impact, instead of a harmful or negative impact? This brings us to . . .

ACT 5: THE NEW AND IMPROVED VAMPIRE

Have you ever thought to yourself while watching a movie, "I wish these characters were more like me?" You're definitely not alone.

Historically, media—whether books, games, movies, or TV shows—hasn't always been great about representing the many different people in the world, such as people of different races, ethnicities, genders, sexualities, abilities, and so much more. I know, it majorly sucks.

But the good news is that things can change for the better. And that goes for vampire media, too. These days, vampire stories are starting to portray a diverse range of people, including people of color (anyone who belongs to a nonwhite racial group) and the LGBTQ+ community (LGBTQ+ is an acronym for anyone who is lesbian, gay, bisexual, transgender, queer, questioning, intersex, asexual, or aromantic). Representation in vampire media is stepping out into the night!

The first Black Dracula was portrayed by actor William Marshall in the movie *Blacula*, directed by William Crain, a cultural milestone for the 1970s. Other films that featured people of color in starring roles include *Blade* (1998), *Queen of the Damned* (2002), *Ganja and Hess* (1973), and *Cronos* (1993). One film that stands out from the classic vampire narrative, both thematically and culturally, is Ana Lily Amirpour's Iranian vampire western, *A Girl Walks Home Alone at Night* (2014). The film follows a vampire girl who stalks the streets at night on a skateboard and falls in love.

For the queer community, there have always been hints of queer-coded vampires, like Lestat and Louis from *Interview with the Vampire* (1994) and Countess Marya Zaleska from *Dracula's Daughter* (1936)—but now they're out and proud! Films such as *Bit* (2019) and *Black as Night* (2021) feature openly queer vampire characters.

Remember *Carmilla*? Based on the novella of the same name, the Canadian web series *Carmilla* launched in August 2014. In the web series, Laura is a university student who is assigned a mysterious new roommate named Carmilla, whom (spoiler alert) she eventually falls in love with. Queer vampires have even made their debut in cartoons: Marceline the Vampire Queen from *Adventure Time* is a cool bass-playing vampire who doesn't drink blood . . . she only drinks the color red! This popular character is voiced by singer and actress Olivia Olson.

Read All About It

Vampire stories aren't restricted to YA lit and adult fiction. Vampire books that fall into the kid lit category include the Amelia Fang series by Laura Ellen Anderson, *Vampires Don't Wear Polka Dots* by Debbie Dadey and Marcia Thornton Jones, *Bunnicula* by Deborah and James Howe, *Rules for Vampires* by Alex Foulkes, *Serwa Boateng's Guide to Vampire Hunting* by Roseanne A. Brown, *The Vanquishers* by Kalynn Bayron, and *Fake Blood* by Whitney Gardner. (And if you would like to branch out into young adult literature, check out the YA anthology of vampire short stories *Vampires Never Get Old: Tales with Fresh Bite* edited by Natalie C. Parker and Zoraida Córdova!)

As kids (and yes, as adults, too), we want to see ourselves and people like us represented in our favorite movies and books. One thing I love about stories is how you can travel the world, have fantastic adventures, and save the day, all with the power of your imagination. Want to be a vampire hunter? Or, on the flip side, want to live in a big Gothic castle and be a vampire? In fiction, you can! When you see yourself as a part of the world and the hero of your story—whether that's in fiction or real life—you know that anything and everything is possible.

As you can tell, vampire stories have changed with the times. Just like vampire legends and myths in the past, modern vampire media can tell us a lot about our values, beliefs, fears, likes, and dislikes as a society.

Take the movie *Vampires vs. the Bronx* (2020), directed by Oz Rodriguez. The film features a group of kids who are fighting to protect their neighborhood from gentrification—that's when a neighborhood changes due to wealthy people moving in, leading to rising costs and unaffordable rent and eventually pushing the original residents out. When vampires show up, the kids have to fight against them, too, to prevent the vampires from draining their community dry—literally and figuratively. While vampires may not show up in your neighborhood, gentrification is very real. If you're due for a movie night, check out this movie!

Vampires themselves may not have a reflection you can see in the mirror, but vampire stories have always reflected the world around us, even as the world changes. Vampire stories can channel some of our deepest fears and speak to our wildest imaginations, whether that's through virus vampires or sparkly bloodsuckers, or even muppets that love to count. And in the future, who knows? I think it's a safe bet to say that vampire stories will continue to reflect the story of humans for many, many, many years to come.

Read All About It

The Library of Alexandria stood tall in Alexandria, Egypt, between approximately 283 BCE and 275 CE. It was the largest library in the world! It contained over 400,000 scrolls made from papyrus. Over the years, the library witnessed Julius Caesar's occupation of Alexandria in 48 BCE, experienced gradual decay and decline thanks to the ravages of time, and had scrolls stolen and damaged. In a final blow, the Roman emperor Diocletian's army occupied the city in 297 CE, during which he reportedly said he would "set fire to the city and burn it completely." Sadly, nothing remains of the library. But there's good news—the Bibliotheca Alexandrina, which opened in 2002, is a hub of learning in Alexandria today.

LIBRARY
I Can't Believe It's NOT Blood
False Blood
DAYLIGHT MOON
THE DENTIST VAMPIRE
THE DENTIST VAMPIRE
Dogicula
Dogicula

WAIT, SO ARE VAMPIRES REAL?

I have never met a vampire personally, but I don't know what might happen tomorrow.

—Bela Lugosi

Vampires, burial, death: inter the corpse where the road forks, so that when it springs from the grave, it will not know which path to follow. . . . The monster is born only at this metaphoric crossroads, as an embodiment of a certain cultural moment—of a time, a feeling, and a place.

—Thesis I: The Monster's Body Is a Cultural Body, from "Monster Culture (Seven Theses)" by Jeffrey Jerome Cohen

Take a deep breath, drink some water, and pat yourself on the back. You've made it to the very end of this guide. But alas, "parting is such sweet sorrow," as Juliet from that famous Shakespeare play once said.

Oh! You have one last question? Ah, yes. The big question that's been hanging over our heads like a vampire bat taking a nap. Are vampires real? Well, dear reader, the answer is still yes . . . and no.

WHAT! SO, VAMPIRES AREN'T REAL?!

I know, I know! You're waving your arms, saying, "What was all this even for if they're not real? Are vampires going to suck my blood or not?!" First of all, rest easy. No vampire is going to suck your blood. You've learned enough skills and you possess enough know-how to deal with the undead like a pro supernaturalist.

Here's the thing, brave reader. Vampires may not be real-real in the way that you might have read in a book or seen in a movie, but I wanted to show you that, even though vampires are the stuff of myths and legends, their stories come from real history and culture.

Think about it! We've dug deep into ancient history, studied up on science, and read about vampire lit, all to build up your vampire expertise! You met bloodsuckers from around the world, learned how to bake mouthwatering garlic bread, and absolutely crushed it at Vampires 101. You've cracked the secret of the European vampire panic. We've even dusted off the coffins of Vlad the Impaler and Bram Stoker for some exclusive interviews!

Most importantly, you've discovered what makes vampires just so fascinating and relevant today. You've seen one fantastic, spooky, and bloodthirsty example of how myths and legends shape (and are shaped by!) our world, our history, our culture, and even ourselves.

UH . . . NOW WHAT?

That's the question for you, my friend—can I call you friend? I feel like we've been through so much together! I've taught you a lot about vampires, but the world of vampires is so much bigger than this little guide. If you want to learn even more, you can! Just get out there and keep reading, observing, and learning.

Want to know how I became a guide to the supernatural? I'll let you in on a little secret. It's not about cool vampire-slaying weapons or being the toughest and scariest. It's about being open to new ideas and learning about the unknown. Knowledge is a powerful thing, after all. And as Spider-Man's uncle once said, "With great power comes great responsibility."

What will you do with your power?

BIBLIOGRAPHY

*Here lie the sources consulted in the writing of
this guide to the world of vampires.*

Bane, Theresa. *Encyclopedia of Vampire Mythology*. Jefferson, NC: McFarland & Company, Inc., Publishers, 2020.

Beccia, Carlyn. *Monstrous: The Lore, Gore, and Science Behind Your Favorite Monsters*. Minneapolis: Lerner Publishing Group, 2019.

Beresford, Matthew. *From Demons to Dracula: The Creation of the Modern Vampire Myth*. London: Reaktion Books, 2008.

Bunson, Matthew. *The Vampire Encyclopedia*. New York: Crown Trade Paperbacks, 1993.

Eldridge, Alison. "Vampire." *Encyclopedia Britannica*. Accessed May 29, 2022. https://www.britannica.com/topic/vampire.

Gross, Emma Starer. "In West Africa, the Adze Is an Insectoid Source of Misfortune." *Atlas Obscura*. October 26, 2020. Accessed May 29, 2022. https://www.atlasobscura.com/articles /monster-mythology-adze.

Kröger, Lisa, and Melanie R. Anderson. *Monster, She Wrote: The Women Who Pioneered Horror and Speculative Fiction*. Philadelphia: Quirk Books, 2019.

Le Fanu, Joseph Sheridan. *Carmilla*. Edited by Carmen Maria Machado. Philadelphia: Lanternfish Press, 2019.